KIDDIE
Cocktails

To Jackson, Hailey and Jenna for making life a little sweeter every day! — *Stuart*

A multitude of gratitude to Eden, Dean n' Emma...I dig you cats the MOST! — *Derek*

Korero Press Ltd, 157 Mornington Road, London, E11 3DT, UK

www.koreropress.com

First published in Great Britain in 2014
Paperback edition published in Great Britain in 2021

© Korero Press Limited

ISBN-13: 978-1-912740-15-4

A CIP catalogue record is available from the British Library

Text by Stuart Sandler; www.misterretro.com

Illustrations by Derek Yaniger; www.derekart.com

Fonts by Font Diner; www.fontdiner.com

Printed in China

KIDDIE Cocktails

by **Stuart Sandler**

illustrations by **Derek Yaniger**

foreword by **Charles Phoenix**

KORERO PRESS

TABLE OF CONTENTS

Foreword

When I was growing up, my family often went out for dinner. It was always a special occasion, but when my grandparents joined us, it was a really special occasion. It became a slightly more formal, dressier affair — the pace became slower, with time for just drinking and socializing, as opposed to getting your drink with dinner. And my grandparents always ordered a kiddie cocktail for me and my brother. Back then, if you were a boy, you'd have a Roy Rogers and if you were a girl you'd have a Shirley Temple. Sometimes even the boys would have a Shirley Temple!

I've always loved soda pop. Some of my earliest memories are of visiting my dad's car lot in downtown Ontario, California, where my brother and I would each get a dime and we'd walk next door to the old liquor store. They had one of those old refrigerated soda pop cases that opened from the top — you'd reach down inside it to grab your soda. I remember my favorite was Orange Crush, and to this day, I still love Orange Crush!

As we got into our junior high school years, we'd go to the 7-11 soda fountain, where you could go from fountain to fountain, mixing up soda pop and creating your own blends. And now that we're older, the sky is the limit!

A few years back, I hosted an event at Galco's, my local soda pop shop in LA, and the world's greatest. I'd bought soda pop there regularly through the years, and they finally asked me to host an event. I love the wide variety of soda pops now available, and I love mixing them together to create what I call Poptails.

Galco's loved the idea of Poptails, so the owner John and I picked a bunch of soda pops to mix together. However, we were very surprised by how long it took us to get two bold color soda pops that could be mixed together to create not only a great color but a great flavor, too. It's not as easy as you'd imagine to get a divine color and flavor result. I couldn't believe how many soda pops clash — I was expecting them all to go together beautifully.

Finally, we settled on the three Poptails we wanted to serve. The day of the event came, and, much to the glee, delight and deep satisfaction of the patrons of all ages, it was a great success. It was a delight to watch them

experiencing their first Poptail! So, when it comes to creating your own Poptails, or kiddie cocktails, I'd say: just Go for it! Be Creative! Have Fun! Get Wild! Get Crazy! Go to the craft store! Unleash your inner crafter on your garnishes! They can be food, they can be feathers. You can have meat! You can have a garnish on a glass that's two feet tall, and if you can balance it, it's doable! You can do anything, really...

Charles Phoenix

Charles Phoenix is a performer, humorist, chef, and author. In his live shows, media appearances and books, the self-proclaimed "retro daddy" explores America's classic and kitschy pop cultural past and present.

Introduction

Back in 1984, when I was 10 years old, my family and I were living in a quiet suburb surrounding Youngstown, Ohio, called Boardman. My brothers and I used to ride our bikes around the neighborhood, usually ending up at the video arcade, where we'd lose the afternoon and a pocket of quarters to our favorite games. When I wasn't outside playing with my brothers or friends, I was busy enjoying my favorite hobby: creating BASIC programs on my IBM personal computer.

That year, every song on the radio was perfection, and I felt pretty cool, out and about in my red multi-zipper Michael Jackson jacket. And my moon walk was proper! I knew even then that 1984 would be one of the best years in my life, and it turns out it was! Sometimes, when I reflect on that year, it's difficult to remember it as anything more than a blur, but there are some clear moments that are forever stuck in my brain. And among those memories, my favorite is about the time I enjoyed my very first kiddie cocktail.

As a kid I was pretty lucky since my family would enjoy a dinner out a few times a week, and when a trip to Jay's Famous Hot Dogs, Cornersburg Pizza, or Arby's wasn't on the menu, we'd occasionally head out for something more exotic — usually in a sit-down restaurant with the lights dimmed for atmosphere.

On one of these occasions in 1984, we headed to the best Chinese restaurant in town — Dragon Palace. It was a particular favorite of my parents, and if the timing was right,

The Dragon Palace Restaurant in Youngstown, Ohio · Image courtesy of Google, Inc.

we'd run into a local television celebrity enjoying his or her dinner, or see some pals from school.

Dinner at the Dragon Palace was always a wonderful ritual, and one I still recall fondly. We'd all start with a bowl of delicious wonton soup, complete with crispy, colorful shrimp chips, which would crackle the moment they hit the soup. That would be followed by an order of egg rolls with a delicious sweet and sour sauce that filled my mouth with a wonderful texture and combination of flavors.

Then we'd enjoy the main course. Mom always ordered egg foo yung and dad ordered pepper steak, which we'd all share, along with my favorite pork fried rice. If we kids were well behaved, and members of the clean plate club, at the end of the meal we'd enjoy rainbow sherbet and each receive a fortune cookie. The food was always wonderful, and we always enjoyed a hot oolong tea with our meal, but that evening, something happened that changed me forever.

As the waiter came to take our drinks order, my mind was clearly somewhere else and I couldn't decide what I wanted to drink with my meal. He looked at me and asked, "Shirley Temple?" I stared back blankly for a moment and then looked at my dad for confirmation. In an effort to move the ordering process along, he answered "Yes" for me and off the waiter went to fetch our drinks.

When he returned, a small clear glass landed on the placemat just in front of my spot. It was filled with a bright red, fizzy liquid, ice cubes, a maraschino cherry on the top that was lanced with a small yellow plastic sword to hold it on the rim of the glass, and a black straw. Small bubbles of carbonation were dancing up the inside of the glass, and making a low sizzle as they reached the top of it. I started by eating the sweet cherry off the sword, as I'd enjoyed these on ice-cream sundaes many times before, but never in a drink.

I raised my glass and leaned in for a taste of my Shirley Temple. Then, all at once, my mouth was full of the most amazing sweet and brilliant flavor I'd ever known at that point in my young life. I could taste the sugary sweet cherry juice and the spice of the ginger in my ginger ale as the bubbles tickled my nose and the small ice cubes tapped my front teeth. I tried my best to savor every sip, but before the meal

arrived I'd exhausted the entire glass. Our soups arrived, and moments later, without anyone asking, another Shirley Temple arrived at our table — much to my delight! I made a point of thanking the waiter many times, and even bowed to him in the hope of expressing my sincere appreciation — much to his puzzled delight.

Remembering my first kiddie cocktail always puts a huge smile on my face. I hope that you will have the same experience with one of the recipes in this book, and that you'll always share your cocktails in the company of family and good friends. Be sure to read through each recipe a few times, and have all the ingredients and tools ready. With any drink, if you find the flavor isn't to your taste, tweak the recipe until you've perfected it before serving. Above all, have fun making, serving, and drinking your kiddie cocktails! After all, life is sweet, but it's really sweet with a kiddie cocktail!

Are you ready?
Let's Get Started!

Setting Up

YOUR BAR

Getting equipped with the right tools and ingredients will ensure your kiddie cocktails are perfectly satisfying every time! Before we head to the supermarket, though, let's learn about the items you'll need to make your kiddie cocktail bar complete!

Cocktail Shaker

The cocktail shaker is a very handy tool. Use one when a recipe calls for it — it's great for deeply mixing your kiddie cocktail ingredients, and for cooling your drink down to a very frosty temperature in a jiffy! Below are the two most popular types.

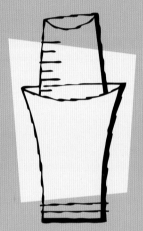

Boston Shaker

This simple, two-piece shaker consists of a metal cup with an inverted glass on top. It works very well, but requires a strainer when you're ready to pour the drink. Be sure to hold the shaker tight when shaking, to avoid a big mess, and for Pete's sake, don't try this with two ordinary cups — it just won't work!

Cobbler Shaker

This is the classic-looking shaker. It consists of three stainless steel parts — one to hold the drink ingredients, another to strain them, and a small cap to seal the drink while you shake it. The Cobbler is easier to shake with than the Boston, but once it gets cold, it's a bear to take apart.

Pitcher

If you decide to double or triple a kiddie cocktail recipe, you'll need a large pitcher to hold your mixed drinks! Any kitchen pitcher or jug will do, and bonus points if it has a lid to keep the flies from sippin'!

Blender

You'll need an electric blender to make the frozen and slush drinks in this book, and it can also be used to make crushed ice. Always pour the liquid in before you add any ice, to keep the blades inside from getting dulled too quickly. And never use a blender without a grown-up's help.

In order to prepare your kiddie cocktails, you'll need the best tools for the job! Chances are you already have these in your home!

Measuring Shot Glass

This has small lines all around it — often in different units of measure and measurement systems. Use it when you need to measure liquids in smaller increments or different systems!

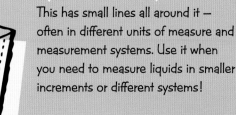

Hawthorne Strainer

If you use a Boston shaker, you'll need to hold one of these over it when you're ready to pour your shaken kiddie cocktail into its serving glass. It'll stop the ice inside the shaker from coming through.

Barspoon

Use one of these long-handled spoons for stirring drinks, as well as for floating ingredients to make layered drinks!

Measuring Spoons

If you've ever made cookies, you've probably used measuring spoons! They are available in many sizes, including tablespoon (tbsp, or just t) and ½ tablespoon, teaspoon (tsp, or just t), and ½ teaspoon.

Double Jigger

This double-sided cup is used to measure and pour liquid ingredients. Typically, the bigger cup holds 1½ oz and the smaller one ¾ oz, but there's also a "pony" jigger that holds 1 oz and ½ oz, and we recommend that for making most of the recipes in this book.

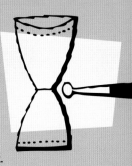

Ice Bucket

Use an ice bucket and tongs whenever you mix cocktails at a party — it'll save you multiple trips to the freezer for more ice! Also, when making drinks, never touch the ice with your hands — that's what the tongs are for!

Mixing Glass

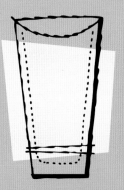

Use a pint glass to thoroughly mix your drink ingredients in with a barspoon before pouring them into their proper serving glass. Hold a Hawthorne Strainer over your pint glass to strain your stirred drink into its proper serving glass.

Glassware

Each kiddie cocktail should always be served in an appropriate glass: below are the glasses that we use in our recipes.

Cocktail Glass

Hurricane Glass

Collins Glass

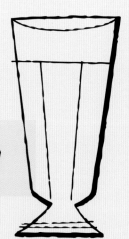

Fountain Glass

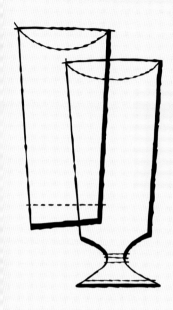

Highball Glass

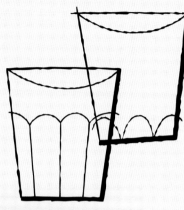

Old Fashioned or Rocks Glass

Margarita Glass

Tumbler Glass

Stocking Your Bar!

To make the best-tasting drinks, always be sure to use the freshest ingredients!

Sodas

7 Up or Sprite, Ginger Ale, Tonic Water, Cola, Soda Water. Always use these well chilled!

Cream of Coconut

This is a thick, rich, sweet white cream made from coconut milk.

Bitters

Like vanilla extract, bitters are alcohol infused with plant extracts. They are used in small amounts to add flavor.

Sour Mix

This tangy, premade mix of lemon, lime, and sugar will give your drinks zing!

Fruit Juices

Lemon, Orange, Pineapple, Cranberry, Lime, Grapefruit. Use fresh squeezed if possible.

Grenadine

This thick, sweet red syrup adds color and flavor. No cherries here, it's made from pomegranate!

Lemonade

Buy this ready made, or mix equal parts lemon juice and white sugar and add water to taste!

Light Cream

Our recipes use cream with 20% or higher milk fat content. Try half and half or whipping cream!

Simple Syrup

Use this like sugar to sweeten your drinks! With a grown-up, put 12 oz of water in a pan and bring it to the boil. Then slowly add 12 oz of white sugar, and stir constantly until dissolved. Take the pan off the heat and allow the syrup to cool and thicken before pouring it into a sealable bottle. It'll stay fresh for about 3 weeks in the fridge.

All About Ice!

To look and taste exactly as it is intended to, each kiddie cocktail requires its own special kind of ice. This might seem odd, but using the wrong kind of ice can actually ruin your drink, and we don't want to waste ingredients!

Ice Cubes

Make these by filling ice cube trays with water and putting them in the freezer. Ice cubes are perfect when you want to shake or serve a drink without diluting its flavor, as they melt more slowly than other types of ice.

Cracked Ice

You'll use this when you need to blend a drink in a blender or a glass, or when ice cubes are too big. Ask a grown-up to help you make it. Wrap some ice cubes in a towel and crush them into pebble-sized pieces with a mallet (or a similar heavy, blunt object).

Crushed Ice

Often confused with cracked ice, crushed ice is the smallest kind of ice. It's used in the preparation of the slush drinks in this book. To make it, follow the instructions for making cracked ice, but continue until the ice pieces are very small.

19

Measuring Cocktails

Double Jigger

Use a double jigger — either a 1½ ounce and ¾ ounce one, or a 1 ounce and ½ ounce pony jigger — to quickly and accurately measure the liquid ingredients shown in ounces in this book.

Measuring Spoons

These are handy for measuring a precise amount of a liquid ingredient (like lemon juice) or a dry one (like sugar). Use them whenever a recipe in this book calls for tablespoon or teaspoon measures.

When making kiddie cocktails, it's very important to follow the recipe and make sure you measure each ingredient you add carefully! Below are the measuring tools you'll need to make your kiddie cocktails tasty and perfect every time! Keep in mind that measuring takes lots of practice and a steady hand!

Measuring Shot Glass

Use one of these instead of a jigger to measure between ½ an ounce and 1½ ounces in ¼ ounce increments.

MIXING TECHNIQUES

BUILDING

Building is the most common method for mixing your kiddie cocktails! When you follow a recipe, add the ingredients in the order given, adding one ingredient right on top of the other until you've got one tasty liquid sandwich! It's OK if the ingredients combine while you're building your drink — it'll still taste the same!

LAYERING
(AKA FLOATING)

Layering is a very tricky technique, and it requires practice and a steady hand! Unlike Building, where you're adding one ingredient at a time and they mix, when you layer a kiddie cocktail, you don't want the ingredients to combine, but to sit in separate layers. To do this, first take the ingredient with the highest sugar content and pour it gently over the back of a barspoon into the serving glass. Then add the other ingredients in the same way — each layer on top of the previous layer — until the drink looks like a stack!

BLENDING

When a kiddie cocktail recipe calls for blending, you'll need an electric blender, and a grown-up to help! Simply combine all your ingredients in the machine, including ice if it's asked for, and blend until smooth and creamy. Then pour the mixture into your serving glass.

ROLLING

Rolling a kiddie cocktail is fun, and looks pretty impressive to your guests! To roll your drink, fill a cocktail shaker with the recipe ingredients, and ice if called for, then pour this mixture into a tall glass. Continue to pour the cocktail between the shaker and the glass about 6 times. Finally, strain it and serve!

STIRRING

If you've ever stirred hot cocoa with a spoon, you're already a professional at stirring! To stir a kiddie cocktail, combine all the ingredients, and ice if the recipe calls for it, in a serving glass and stir with a barspoon.

SHAKING

Shaking is the best way to quickly mix and chill any kiddie cocktail! Always use a cocktail shaker when shaking, instead of two inverted cups, to prevent a liquid mess! To shake, pour your ingredients into the shaker and seal it well. Give it ten good shakes before straining the drink into a serving glass!

23

Cocktail Garnishes

Fruit Wedge

There are no rules when it comes to garnishing your drinks! Garnishes add a pop of color and flavor!

Parasol

Fruit Slice

Strawberry

Mint Sprig

Citrus Twist

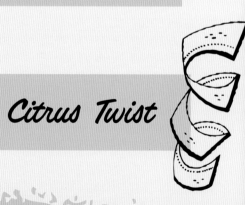

Cocktail Sword

Cocktail Pick

Swizzle Stick

Whipped Cream

Fruit Wheel

Maraschino Cherries

How to Host a...

KIDDIE

COCKTAIL

PARTY

Once you've gathered up all your barware, glasses, and ingredients, and have mastered the recipes in this book, it's time to throw your very own kiddie cocktail party! To make your party a smashing success, we've prepared a ten-point checklist to help get you organized before the day, plus some great ideas for music to play and food to serve!

Visit our website — www.kiddiecocktails.com — to find a printable checklist and invitation templates, plus lots more suggestions for music, food, and decorations. These will help you get your party started out right!

We know you're chompin' at the bit to get going, so make sure you spend time reading and thinking about each item on the party checklist on pages 30–31, only moving on to the next item once you've completed the previous one!

Festive Food!

Looking for the perfect snacks to serve with your kiddie cocktails? Look no further! Nothing complements the sweet, fizzy taste of a kiddie cocktail like one of these tasty salty snacks:

- Potato Chips · Pretzels · Peanuts · Cereal Mix · Corn Chips
- Crackers · Popcorn · Puffed Cheeseballs · Tortilla Chips

In the mood for something more savory? Try these tasty morsels:

- Veggies & Dips · Hot Dogs · Hamburgers · Deli Meats · Cheese
- Nachos · Pizza · Pizza Rolls · Meatballs · Chili · Egg Rolls

Stereo-Fi

Nothing gets the party started faster than good music, and we've got the perfect playlist! Take a listen to some of these great recording artists!

1950s Lounge Music

Dean Martin, Frank Sinatra, Nat King Cole, Louis Prima, Perry Como, Sammy Davis Jr., Sam Butera, Bobby Darin, Sonny King, Matt Monro

1960s Surf Music

The Beach Boys, Dick Dale, The Ventures, Davie Allan, The Chantays, Jan & Dean, Ricky Dean, The Surf Teens, The Tornados, The Challengers

Rockabilly Music

Stray Cats, Gene Vincent, Eddie Cochran, Roy Orbison, Elvis Presley, Duane Eddy, Buddy Holly, Jerry Lee Lewis, Polecats, Carl Perkins

Tiki Exotica Music

Esquivel, Les Baxter, Martin Denny, Arthur Lyman, Robert Drasnin, Chaino, Morton Gould, Xavier Cugat, Sergio Mendes, Pérez Prado

1950s Doo Wop

The Ink Spots, The Mills Brothers, The Ravens, The Platters, Frankie Lymon and the Teenagers, Dion & the Belmonts, The Four Seasons

1960s Bubblegum Pop

1910 Fruitgum Company, The Ohio Express, The Archies, Tommy Roe, Bobby Sherman, The Monkees, Herman's Hermits

29

Party Checklist!

☑ **Choose your Party Theme**

Will it be Spage Age? Tiki Exotica? International Spy? There are so many wonderful themes you could choose for your kiddie cocktail party, you may have a hard time selecting just one!

☑ **Send your Party Invitations**

Once you've chosen a theme, it's time to create your party invitations. Send them within 2–3 weeks of your party. Need help? Download invitation templates from www.kiddiecocktails.com

☑ **Party Location and Seating**

Think about the best place to hold your party, and about how you'd like to set up the room or space. Make sure there are enough seats for all your guests to sit and relax!

☑ **Party Activities**

Plan to have a few games and activities for your guests to enjoy while you're busy whipping up cocktails! Find plenty of great suggestions at www.kiddiecocktails.com!

☑ **Select your Cocktails**

If you're inviting a very large group, serve a punch while folks wait for you to mix their kiddie cocktails. Also, choose a few featured cocktails to serve, plus a few you can make on request!

Planning and preparation are the keys to hosting a fun and successful kiddie cocktail party! Work your way through the checklist to make sure you've considered every detail of your party, and shop for ingredients, food, and decorations well in advance. That way, you'll be able to enjoy the party too!

☑ Decorations & Music

On the day of the party, decorate your space according to your theme — make it lively and inviting! Ask a grown-up to help you set up the music! Check out our suggestions on the previous page.

☑ Dress for Success

Once the room is decorated, it's time to get dressed! Be sure to dress appropriately, according to your theme. Whatever you choose, make it comfortable, as you'll be busy making cocktails!

☑ Food, Plates & Napkins

A party isn't complete without hors d'oeuvres (pronounced or-durves). Buy some snacks to serve and have plenty of plates and napkins on hand! Set these out 30 minutes before party time.

☑ Garnishes, Cups & Ice

With the help of a grown-up, cut up your fruit garnishes, fill your ice bucket, and get your cups and kiddie cocktail bar ready! Leave fizzy beverages in the fridge till just before party time!

☑ Welcome your Guests

What's that sound? It's the doorbell announcing the arrival of your guests! Be sure to greet everyone at the door with a big smile, and let them know how happy you are to have them at your party!

Classic
COCKTAILS

In the years since the very first kiddie cocktail first touched young lips, only a few drinks have become classics that have endured the test of time. Each of the following drinks has its own personality, yet all retain a perfect balance between sweet and sour — with just a touch of fizz! Enjoy!

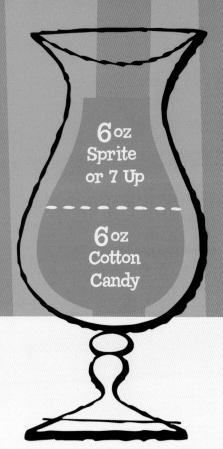

6 oz Sprite or 7 Up

6 oz Cotton Candy

COTTON CANDY

So simple and so tasty you may not be able to stop yourself from drinking it! Stuff a hurricane glass full of cotton candy and slowly pour chilled Sprite or 7 Up over the top. Watch the cotton candy melt, then top it off with a handful of ice cubes. Enjoy through a tall straw.

P*INK ROYALE

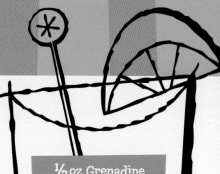

½ oz Grenadine

1 oz Sprite or 7 Up

1 oz Lemon Juice

2 oz Pineapple Juice

2 oz Orange Juice

You'll feel like royalty as you sip this delicate pink nectar! Fill a collins or highball glass halfway with ice cubes, then add the fruit juices and the other ingredients.

Give the drink a hearty stir until it turns a beautiful pink color, then garnish it with a lemon slice and serve!

The Shirley Temple

"The Original Kiddie Cocktail"

½ oz Grenadine

8 oz Ginger Ale

Named for the famous curly-headed child actress of the 1930s and '40s, this is served across the country as America's most popular kiddie cocktail. Serve in a highball glass half filled with ice cubes and garnish with a maraschino cherry!

S.S. LOLLIPOP

Texas Tumbleweed

4 oz Tonic Water

6 oz Orange Juice

Yeehaw! Get ready for this tasty lone star state treat, pardner. This is sure to put hair on your chest and a swagger in your step! Serve in a highball glass half filled with ice cubes and garnish it with a lime slice.

Cactus Juice

Strap on your stetson for this tangy treat! Those brave enough to sample this tasty cactus nectar will feel a sour sensation roll over their tongue like a desert wind.

Build in an old fashioned glass half filled with cracked ice, and garnish with a lime slice. Add a dash of Tabasco sauce to make it prickly!

1/2 oz Lime Juice

2 oz Sprite or 7 Up

2 oz Sour Mix

The Roy Rogers
"King of Kiddie Cocktails"

Named after Hollywood's "King of the Cowboys," Roy Rogers, this was created in the 1940s as a variation on the Shirley Temple for little buckaroos and became an instant classic. Today it's certain to trip your Trigger!

Serve in a highball glass half filled with ice cubes. Garnish with a maraschino cherry and a lemon slice.

1oz Grenadine

8oz Cola

The Egg Cream

Get your mitts on this tasty Brooklyn, New York, original!

Pour the milk into a fountain glass, then top it with the soda water. Stir briskly until foamy. Add the chocolate syrup, stir, and serve immediately.

1oz Chocolate Syrup

6oz Soda Water

4oz Milk 2% or Higher

The Pussyfoot

2oz
Grapefruit Juice

2oz
Pineapple Juice

2oz
Orange Juice

½oz
Grenadine

There's no tiptoeing around it, the Pussyfoot is the fruitasticly tasty customer you've been thirsting for!

Build all the ingredients in a footed highball glass partly filled with cracked ice, then stir. Garnish with fresh fruit, a cherry and a straw, and serve!

Virgin Mary

The story of Virgin Mary is as mysterious as it is legendary. There was once a peaceful kingdom threatened by an angry dragon who scared the villagers. The king's daughter, Mary, was so brave, she confronted the dragon and learned he was sad because he could no longer breathe fire. To rekindle the dragon's fire, Mary created a special spicy potion to restore it, bringing peace throughout the land.

6 drops Worcestershire Sauce

4 oz Tomato Juice

3 drops Tabasco Sauce

Juice of **1** Lemon Wedge

1 pinch Black Pepper

1 pinch Celery Salt

BEWARE HOT!

Many years later, Mary's potion was re-created as the Virgin Mary kiddie cocktail and served in New York City.

Serve in a highball or rocks glass and garnish with a stalk of celery, a pickle spear, a strip of bacon, a spear of asparagus, or all of 'em!

41

The Nada Colada

Put the pineapple juice, cream of coconut, and a glass of crushed ice in a blender and blend at high speed until smooth.

Pour into a hurricane glass and garnish with a maraschino cherry and a pineapple wedge. Serve immediately!

2 oz
Cream
of Coconut

7 oz
Pineapple
Juice

BUMP

Strawberry Daiquiri

Taste that Caribbean breeze with this sweet treat! Put a glass of cracked ice in a blender and then add the strawberries, lime juice, and sugar. Blend until smooth and pour into a cocktail glass. Garnish with a strawberry or an orange slice.

2oz Orange Juice

2oz Cranberry Juice

1 tbsp Grenadine

1oz Peach Nectar

3oz Frozen Strawberries in Syrup (or Fresh)

2 tsp White Sugar

1oz Lime Juice

Fun On the Beach

Get that sweet Summertime flavor in a glass! Mix the orange and cranberry juice in a cocktail glass, then add the peach nectar. Add the grenadine and watch it sink to the bottom. Then garnish with a pineapple wedge and serve!

The Blue Blizzard

Get ready for this tasty Arctic treat, topped with a heaping glacier of ice cream! Feel the cool flavor whip through your mouth like a polar wind!

Combine the drink mix, Sprite or 7 Up, and white cranberry juice in a hurricane glass. Give it a taste and stir in sugar to your liking. Top with a scoop of vanilla ice cream and give it a few stirs to make a blizzard in your glass!

1 scoop
Vanilla
Ice Cream

½ tsp
Blue Kool
Aid Mix

¼ tsp
White Sugar

4 oz
Sprite
or 7 Up

4 oz
White Cranberry
Juice

THE CHOMP

Mix the lemon juice, bitters, and grenadine in a collins glass half filled with cracked ice. Finish off with the ginger ale and garnish with an orange slice! 1-Up!

8 oz Ginger Ale

2 tsp Lemon Juice

1 tsp Grenadine

4 drops Bitters

45

The Arnie Palmer

FORE!

3 oz Lemonade

6 oz Iced Tea

Considered by some to be the most refreshing beverage in the world, this was invented in the mid 1970s by US golfing legend Arnold Palmer. Served in a tall glass half filled with ice cubes, garnish with a lemon wedge and serve.

Wavebender

Hang ten and grab a tasty Wavebender — it's like drinking a sunset in a glass! Start by filling a cocktail shaker halfway with ice cubes then add both juices and the grenadine before shaking well.

Pack a highball glass to the top with ice cubes, then strain the juice mix into the glass. Top it off with ginger ale, stir, and serve ice cold!

5 oz Ginger Ale

½ oz Lemon Juice

1 oz Orange Juice

1 tsp Grenadine

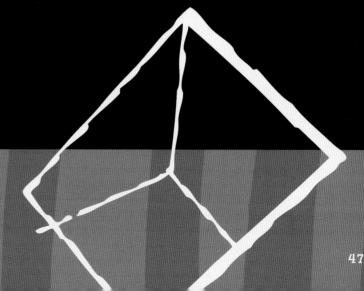

Tropical
COCKTAILS

There's nothing like a delightful tropical kiddie cocktail — they'll sweep you away on a warm Caribbean breeze to exotic destinations! These unique cocktails are blended with a balance of sweetness and paradise, and they'll tickle your mouth with exciting island fruit flavors.

BORA BORA

1½ oz Passion Fruit Juice

2½ oz Pineapple Juice

¼ oz Grenadine

¼ oz Lemon Juice

Get ready for a Tahitian treat from this tropical island! Combine all the ingredients in a cocktail or margarita glass filled with cracked ice, then stir. Garnish with a pineapple wedge and a maraschino cherry.

The LAVA FLOW

Experience a taste of Hawaii with this explosive drink! The secret is to combine two mixes to create real lava in your glass!

Whizz the strawberries and 2 tbsp water in a blender until smooth, then pour into a hurricane glass. Clean the blender, add the other ingredients, blend, and then pour into the strawberry mix. Stir gently and add a straw.

1oz
Light Cream

2½oz
Cream of Coconut

2½oz
Pineapple Juice

4 Frozen
Strawberries

BEACH BLANKET *BINGO

Get your toes in the sand
and relax with this cool number!
Combine the chilled juices in a margarita glass,
top with the soda water and garnish with a lime wedge.

3 oz Grapefruit Juice
3 oz Cranberry Juice
1 oz Soda Water

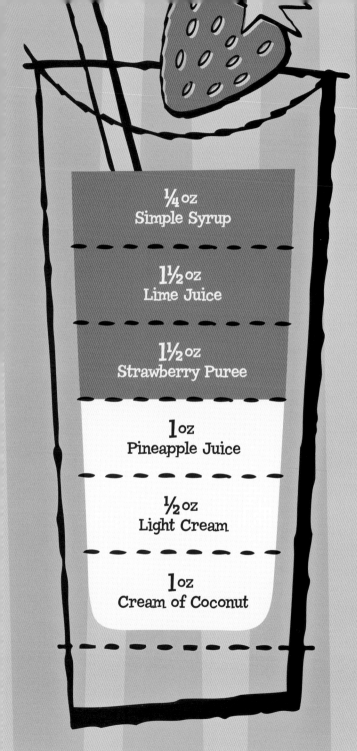

1/4 oz
Simple Syrup

1 1/2 oz
Lime Juice

1 1/2 oz
Strawberry Puree

1 oz
Pineapple Juice

1/2 oz
Light Cream

1 oz
Cream of Coconut

MIAMI NICE

Nothing beats the Miami heat like the coolest duo in town, Miami Nice!

In a blender, combine the pineapple juice, both creams, and a quarter of a highball glass of crushed ice and blend until smooth. Pour the mixture into a clean highball glass and set aside.

Clean the blender, then add the strawberry puree, lime juice, simple syrup, and a quarter of a highball glass of crushed ice and blend until smooth.

Next, float the strawberry mixture on top of the cream mixture by slowly pouring it over the back of a barspoon — keeping the two separated in the glass. Garnish with a strawberry and serve.

THE Flamingo

4 oz Cranberry Juice
2 oz Pineapple Juice
½ oz Lemon Juice
2 oz Soda Water

There's no need to stand on one foot to enjoy this pink drink! In a cocktail shaker half filled with ice cubes, shake the juices then strain them into a highball or cocktail glass. Top off with the soda water, and stir. Garnish with a lime wedge.

Sundowner

4 oz White Grape Juice

1½ oz Soda Water

After the sun sets, make the evening sparkle!
Combine the chilled white grape juice and soda water
in a cocktail glass and garnish with fresh mint leaves.
The longer this drink sits, the more flavorful it becomes!

Fruit Loops

The tangy, sweet, fruity flavors will have you spinning loops!
Mix all the ingredients in a cocktail shaker half filled with
ice cubes and then strain into an old fashioned glass.
Garnish with orange and lemon slices and a cherry.

3 oz Pineapple Juice

1 oz Cranberry Juice

4 drops Grenadine

1½ oz Orange Juice

The BLUE LAGOON

Grab that ukulele and get ready to be the hit of the luau with a cool, citrusy Blue Lagoon! Fill a collins glass to the top with ice cubes, then add the lemonade and blue curaçao syrup. Give the mixture a few stirs until blended. Top it off with your favorite lemon-lime soda and garnish with a cherry or a lemon slice.

6oz
Sprite
or 7 Up

3oz
Lemonade

1oz
Blue Curaçao
Syrup

Lime in de Coconut

In goes the lime, peel and all, to make this tangy tropical drink! Put a glass of crushed ice into a blender, then add all the ingredients, including the entire lime wedge. Blend until smooth, pour into a rocks glass, or a coconut shell, and garnish with a lime wedge.

½ a Lime Wedge

2oz Lime Cordial

1oz Sprite or 7 Up

2oz Cream of Coconut

4oz Pineapple Juice

1oz Orange Juice

2 pinches of Nutmeg

1oz Cream of Coconut

Castaway

This classic tiki drink is sure to lift your spirits! Combine all the ingredients in a cocktail shaker half filled with ice cubes, shake well and strain into a chilled highball glass. Top with nutmeg and garnish with a maraschino cherry or a pineapple slice.

Little Pink Pearl

Enjoy this sweet jewel of the sea! Combine all the ingredients in a cocktail shaker filled halfway with ice cubes. Shake well, then strain into a chilled cocktail glass and garnish with a grapefruit slice.

2 oz Red Grapefruit Juice

½ oz Orgeat Syrup

1 oz Lime Juice

The LIME Rickey

1 oz Simple Syrup
6 oz Soda Water
½ tsp Bitters
¾ oz Lime Juice

Feel the beat with this zesty
number! Build all the ingredients
in a collins glass, then top with
the soda water. Garnish with a
lime twist or wheel and serve.

LIMONADA

7 oz
Soda Water

3 oz
Lime Juice

2 tbsp
White Sugar

Stay cool in the hot Mexican sun with this refreshing, sparkly lime drink! Combine the lime juice and sugar in a tumbler and stir until the sugar has dissolved. Add the soda water and mix gently, then add ice cubes and garnish with a lime wheel.

NOJITO

Refresh, island style, with this swell mint/lime combo! Put the mint leaves, lime juice, and simple syrup in a footed highball glass. Gently mash the ingredients together, being careful not to tear the leaves. Fill the glass with ice cubes, add the soda water, and stir gently to combine. Garnish with a mint sprig and serve!

2 oz
Soda Water

1½ oz
Simple Syrup

3 oz
Lime Juice

8
Mint Leaves

PUNCHBOWL
PARTY

You're invited! Bring your friends along to our punchbowl party! Nothing is finer than a ladle full of sweet and tangy punch! We're sure you won't be disappointed with these wonderful, tongue-tantalizing treats! Come one, come all. Let's dive in!

Orange Sherbet Punch

This zingy orange sherbet punch is the queen of all orange punches! With its bright, citrusy notes and smooth, creamy texture, it's a guaranteed hit at any party! Combine the ginger ale and juices in your punchbowl, then float the scoops of sherbet on top and serve!

16 scoops Orange Sherbet

50oz Ginger Ale

21oz Orange Juice

8oz Pineapple Juice

Classic Punch

Who knew that combining three simple ingredients could produce something so creamy, tangy, and sweet — all at the same time? This basic punch recipe couldn't be simpler or tastier! Start by filling your punchbowl with sherbet, then add the fruit punch and top with chilled Sprite or 7 Up!

16 scoops Strawberry Sherbet

128 oz Fruit Punch

68 oz Sprite or 7 Up

Golden Punch

This isn't your typical punch! Golden Punch is the king of punches, with its bright citrus flavor and refreshing taste! Combine all but the water in your punchbowl, then stir well until mixed. Add the water and stir again till blended, then serve. For a fizzy option, simply replace the water with chilled Sprite or 7 Up.

12 oz Frozen Orange Juice Concentrate

46 oz Pineapple Juice

14 oz Lemon Juice

32 tbsp White Sugar

128 oz Water

Orchard Punch

There's nothing like a tasty apple treat to get you in the mood for Autumn, and this crisp, refreshing Orchard Punch is just the ticket! Simply pour the cranberry juice concentrate, apple juice, and orange juice into your punchbowl and combine them until the concentrate has fully dissolved. Then top up slowly with the chilled ginger ale.

Once the punch is prepared, slice your apple across its waist — revealing the pretty flower patterns of the seed pods. When you have enough slices to cover your punch, gently float them on top of it. Then serve your guests!

12oz Frozen Cranberry Juice Concentrate

22oz Apple Juice

50oz Ginger Ale

8oz Orange Juice

1 tart Red Apple

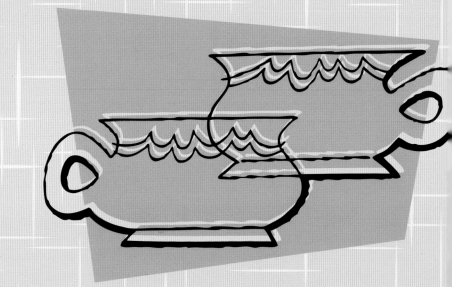

Cardinal Punch

Inspired by the brilliant red bird of the same name, this punch will have you singing with glee through the trees!

Fill a bundt cake pan about halfway with water, then put it in the freezer. Once the water is frozen, you'll have an ice ring, which you can remove by simply setting the pan in water to loosen it. Add the ring to the punchbowl.

Pour the juices into the punchbowl, over the ice ring, and stir gently. Slowly add the chilled ginger ale, then garnish with lemon or orange slices and serve!

32oz Cranberry Juice
128oz Ginger Ale
16oz Orange Juice
4oz Lemon Juice

Planter's Punch

This famous fruity punch owes its origins to the tropical isle of Jamaica, and has become a classic favorite around the globe! In a punchbowl filled with ice cubes, add all the ingredients and stir until well combined. Garnish the punchbowl by floating lemon, lime, and orange slices. Ladle the drink into punch cups filled with ice cubes!

40oz Pineapple Juice

60oz Orange Juice

5oz Lemon Juice

3oz Grenadine

Glow Punch

Lasso the sun, then squeeze its brilliant yellow rays into a bowl, and you've got Glow Punch! This wonderfully tart and sweet punch has a fabulous golden yellow color that will brighten any occasion! In your punchbowl, combine the concentrates and chilled apple juice until well blended. Gently stir in the chilled ginger ale, float the scoops of sherbet on top, serve and enjoy!

6 oz Frozen Lemonade Concentrate

6 oz Frozen Orange Juice Concentrate

32 oz Apple Juice   **64** oz Ginger Ale

4 scoops Lemonade Sherbet

Pilgrim's Punch

Hold the stuffing and the turkey! Grab your buckle hat and enjoy this sweet and sparkling punch!

Fill a bundt cake pan about halfway with water and then put it in the freezer to create an ice ring. Once frozen, simply set the pan in water to loosen the ring, then add it to the punchbowl.

Pour the chilled juices into the punchbowl, over the ice ring, then slowly add the chilled soda water and stir gently. Float the lemon wheels on top of the punch for garnish, and serve your guests!

85oz Soda Water

1 Lemon (Sliced into Wheels)

64oz Grape Juice

64oz Cranberry Juice

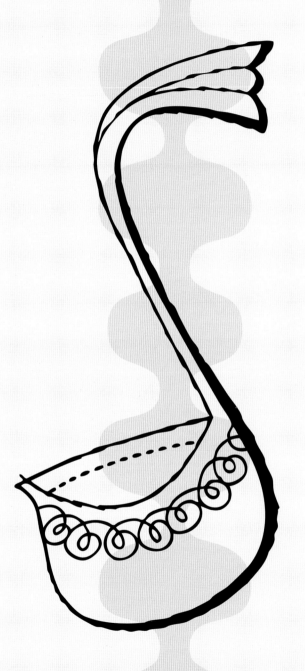

71

Dream Punch

No need to pinch yourself, you're not dreaming — that dreamy flavor you're tasting is the creamy orange Dream Punch!

Put all the frozen ingredients into the punchbowl and let them thaw for 10–15 minutes. Then, slowly stir in the chilled ginger ale. Garnish your punch with frozen orange wheels to keep it cool!

8 scoops Vanilla Ice Cream

16 scoops Orange Sherbet

67 oz Ginger Ale

6 oz Frozen Orange Juice Concentrate

Richard's Reward

Richard was a very good boy! He finished his homework every night, ate all his vegetables happily, and enjoyed his nightly bath! The townspeople were so happy to have such a fine young gentleman in their midst, they threw a party for him for which they prepared a special delicious punch that became known as Richard's Reward!

In a large pot, combine the water, simple syrup, and juices and refrigerate until well chilled.
At serving time, transfer the juice mix to the punchbowl and add the soda water.
Garnish with orange and lemon wheels and serve!

12 oz Orange Juice   **48** oz Cranberry Juice

2 oz Simple Syrup   **2** oz Lemon Juice

48 oz Soda Water   **24** oz Water

Dessert
DRINKS

Once you've eaten all your supper, there's no better way to wash down your peas and carrots than with a tasty dessert drink! These delicious, tongue-tinglingly chilly treats are sure to please — just like an ice-cream sundae in a glass!

Black Cow

The Black Cow was introduced in the late 1800s. To prepare, scoop the ice cream into a chilled mug or a tall parfait glass, then add the root beer and stir to combine.

2 scoops Vanilla Ice Cream

10oz Root Beer

Golden Cow

In Brazil, this is called a vaca dourada: to stay true to the original recipe, follow the Black Cow instructions but replace the root beer with guarana soda. If you can't find this locally, you can purchase it online. Beware though: it's full of caffeine!

Otherwise, for a refreshingly crisp dessert drink with a similar taste, use a sparkling apple juice.

Purple Cow

Don't knock it till you've tried it: the Purple Cow is one tasty customer! Simply follow the Black Cow recipe, replacing the root beer with grape soda.

Brown Cow

Make no mistake my friends, the Brown Cow is one shifty drink — it has no less than three different variations:

Depending on which state they're from, folks in the US also call a Black Cow a Brown Cow.

Some folks swap the vanilla ice cream for chocolate ice cream in their Black Cow!

Others still will fill a mug with two scoops of vanilla ice cream, add 1 oz of chocolate syrup and top it off with 9 oz of Cola! So, how now Brown Cow? The choice is yours!

Pink Cow

Yeehaw! Here's one for the little ladies! Simply follow the Black Cow recipe, but replace the root beer with strawberry soda.

1oz
Lemonade

1oz
Raspberry
Puree

1oz
Grapefruit Juice

1oz
Pineapple Juice

1 Scoop
Orange Sherbet

Summer Rain

You'll be singin' in the rain with this cool and fruity smoothie!
In a blender, combine half a hurricane glass of crushed ice with
all the ingredients except the lemonade, then blend until smooth!
Pour into a clean hurricane glass and top with the lemonade.
Garnish with a citrus fruit wedge and a straw, and serve!

The Pink Squirrel

It's sweet! It's pink! You'll go nutty for another! In a blender, mix all the ingredients together until smooth, then pour into a cocktail glass. Garnish with a maraschino cherry and serve.

2 oz Amaretto Coffee Creamer

½ oz Grenadine

1 scoop Vanilla Ice Cream

THE *Golden Caddie*

Ladies and gentlemen... let us introduce The Golden Caddie! Wait till you lay your hands on this sweet ride! Buckle up and get ready to experience a taste of luxury with your very own Golden Caddie. Start by putting half a glass of crushed ice in a blender, then add the ingredients and blend until smooth. Pour into a cocktail glass and serve!

1 tbsp Chocolate Syrup
1/8 tsp Vanilla Extract
1/8 tsp Anise Extract
2 oz Light Cream
1/2 oz Orange Juice

The Dreamsicle

Whizz all the ingredients together in a blender until smooth, then pour into a chilled footed highball or fountain glass. Garnish with an orange or lime wedge and serve.

2oz Milk, 2% or Higher

2oz Orange Juice

1½ scoops Orange Sherbet

1½ scoops Vanilla Ice Cream

Hawaiian Island Surfer

When you want to taste the flavor of the islands, say "Aloha!" to this creamy treat!

In a blender, combine all the ingredients with a glass of crushed ice and blend until smooth. Pour into a cocktail glass, garnish with citrus fruit wedges and a cherry and serve!

2 scoops Orange Sherbet

1oz Cream of Coconut

2oz Pineapple Juice

2 scoops Vanilla Ice Cream

THE BOSTON COOLER

Invented in Detroit, Michigan, home of Vernors soda, the Boston Cooler was Vernors' answer to the Black Cow. To serve, scoop the ice cream into a tumbler or a tall parfait glass, then add the ginger ale. Stir to combine and serve with a straw!

10oz
**Vernors
Ginger
Ale**

1oz Cream of Coconut
2oz Grapefruit Juice
2oz Pineapple Juice
1oz Light
Cream

ACAPULCO WAVE

Dive into the smooth, rich taste of the tropics! In a cocktail shaker half filled with ice cubes, shake all the ingredients until well blended. Strain into a margarita glass, garnish with a pineapple wedge and a cherry and serve!

5 oz
Peach Nectar

5 oz
Soda Water

3 Peach
Slices

THE PEACH MELBA

Combine the peach slices, peach nectar, and soda water in a highball glass, then top with a scoop of raspberry sherbet and 3 fresh raspberries and serve.

The Grasshopper

2oz Crème de Menthe Syrup

2oz Milk, 2% or Higher

1 Scoop Vanilla Ice Cream

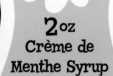

Hop in to minty delight! In a blender, mix all the ingredients together until smooth, then pour into a hurricane glass. Garnish with a dollop of whipped cream and serve with a candy cane!

Elephant Charger

How do you stop an elephant from charging? Take his credit cards, or serve him one of these!

Peel and slice the banana and peach. Add them, and the other ingredients, to a blender and blend until smooth. Pour into a chilled hurricane glass and serve!

2 oz Orange Juice

2 oz Milk, 2% or Higher

1 Ripe Peach

2 oz Raspberries

1 Overripe Banana

2 Scoops Vanilla Ice Cream

Get your tastebuds ready for some of the most tingly, flavorful, and mouth-watering kiddie cocktails you've ever tried! These modern recipes pick up from where the classics left off, and they're out of this world!

ATOMIC CAT

4oz
Tonic Water

3oz
Orange Juice

Dig it! Mix the tonic water and orange juice in a collins glass half filled with ice cubes. Stir and serve, Daddio!

It's WAY OUT! You're gonna dig it the MOST!

BOMB POP!

Celebrate this 4th of July in style with this amazing kiddie cocktail. It's sure to impress your guests and leave 'em wondering how you made it!

The Bomb Pop is served layered — just like a cake — so each ingredient sits on top of the other, not blending together, using a technique called layering (see page 22). The secret to keeping the ingredients separate lies in the amount of sugar in each of 'em!

To start, make sure your ingredients are ice cold from the refrigerator. Then, in a collins glass filled to the top with crushed ice, gently add the cranberry juice.

Next, very slowly and gently, pour the lemonade over the crushed ice, adding more crushed ice as you go. Then repeat with the Gatorade G2. Serve with a straw!

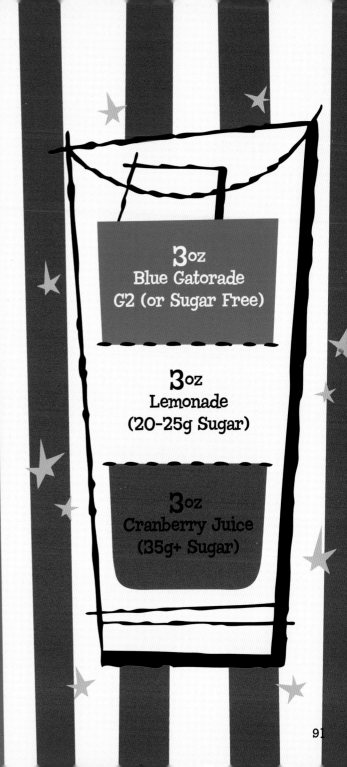

3oz
Blue Gatorade
G2 (or Sugar Free)

3oz
Lemonade
(20-25g Sugar)

3oz
Cranberry Juice
(35g+ Sugar)

Cranberry Pucker

2 oz
Ginger Beer

- - - - - - - -

4 oz
Lemonade

- - - - - - - -

2 oz
Cranberry Juice

There's nothing finer than the taste of sweet and tart cranberries to get your morning going and your mouth watering!

Fill a highball glass to the top with crushed ice, then add the fresh-squeezed lemonade and white cranberry juice. Top off with the ginger beer, stir gently to blend, and serve!

Crabapple

When you're craving the taste of a tart and sour crabapple, nothing can beat this kiddie cocktail! It'll make your toes curl inside your shoes, and you'll be licking your lips for more!

Combine the ingredients in a cocktail shaker half filled with ice cubes, and shake till well blended. Strain into a collins glass half filled with ice cubes and serve with a straw!

2½ oz
Cranberry Juice

- - - - - - - -

2 oz
Apple Juice

- - - - - - - -

½ oz
Simple Syrup

- - - - - - - -

1 oz
Lime Juice

Evil Princess

No eye of newt or lips of toad are required to enjoy this sweet, purple magic potion. It'll put you under its spell!

1 oz Grenadine

1 tbsp Lemon Juice

1 tbsp Vanilla Syrup

1 oz Apple Juice

2 oz Grape Juice

Combine the ingredients in a collins glass half filled with ice cubes, stir well and garnish with a lime slice.

The Yellowjacket

You'll be buzzing with joy, sipping on this tart treat! Pour all the ingredients into a cocktail shaker half filled with ice cubes and shake well. Strain into a rocks glass filled with ice cubes, garnish with a lemon wheel, and serve!

2 oz Pineapple Juice
1½ oz Lemon Juice
2 oz Orange Juice

Windermere

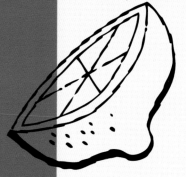

If you ever find yourself in Hong Kong craving ginger, this spicy, refreshing treat is just the ticket! If you can't get your hands on any ginger beer, lemonade will do as a sweet alternative!

Swirl the bitters around the inside of a highball glass to coat, then fill halfway with ice cubes. Add the remaining ingredients, stir gently and serve!

3 oz
Ginger Beer

3 oz
Ginger Ale

½ oz
Lime Juice

8 drops
Bitters

Lemon, Lime & Bitters

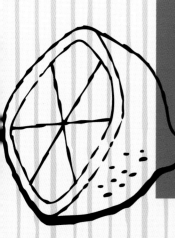

When it gets hot in the Outback, our Australian friends down under know how to keep it cool with a Lemon, Lime & Bitters — or LLB as it's known!

Fill a highball glass with ice cubes, pour the bitters over the ice and swirl around about 5 times to coat the sides of the glass evenly. Next, add the lime juice and top with Sprite or 7 Up. Garnish with slices of lemon and lime and serve!

6 oz
Sprite or 7 Up

½ oz
Lime Juice

2 tsp
Bitters

Get an explosive tang and a wonderful mouth-puckering punch of cherry with the Cherry Bomb! Combine the juices in a cocktail shaker half filled with ice cubes, then shake well and strain into a highball glass filled with cracked ice. Top it off with 7 Up or Sprite, and garnish with a cherry or a lime slice.

½ oz Lime Juice

1 oz Sprite or 7 Up

4 oz
Maraschino
Cherry Juice

THE GREEN ALIEN

2 oz
Sprite or 7 Up

3 oz
Lemonade

3 oz
Lime Juice

It's out of this world! Pour the juices into a cocktail shaker half filled with ice cubes and shake well. Strain into a collins glass filled halfway with cracked ice and top with the 7 Up or Sprite. Add a drop of green coloring and stir. Garnish with a lime slice.

1 Kiwi

1 tbsp
White Sugar

1 oz
Orange Juice

2 oz
Pineapple
Juice

KOSMIC KOOLER

Make the official drink of space at home! In a blender, combine the juices and sugar and mix well. Add a glass of crushed ice and blend until smooth. Slice the kiwi and add that too; pulse until just blended — so as not to crush the seeds. Pour the mixture into a collins glass and garnish with an orange slice.

THE FIZZ

Get your lips ready for this tingly taste sensation: It's time for the Fizz!

Fill a cocktail shaker halfway with ice cubes and add the juices. Shake well, then strain into a chilled highball glass. Top with soda water and serve.

3oz Cranberry Juice

3oz Orange Juice

3oz Soda Water

ELIMARY'S COCKTAIL

2
Raspberries

- - - - - - - -

3oz
Pineapple Juice

- - - - - - - -

1 tsp Grenadine

- - - - - - - -

4oz Lemonade

Plunk! Plunk! Enjoy a refreshing summer cannonball dive into this sweet creation! Start by putting the chilled lemonade into a cocktail glass, then pour in the chilled pineapple juice. Very slowly, pour the grenadine on top, then gently drop in each raspberry, one at a time.

Garnish with a lime wedge, pop in a straw and serve!

BONUS!

SODA MIXING

The next time you find yourself standing in front of a restaurant soda fountain with all those delightful flavors staring back at you, grab a glass and start mixing 'em to create your own custom soda blends! Try our soda recipes or discover your favorite!

Krazy Kombos

¾ Fruit Punch + ¼ Orange Soda = Bubblegum

½ Cream Soda + ½ Cherry Cola = Cherry Pie

⅓ Root Beer + ⅔ Mountain Dew = Mountain Beer

⅓ Cola + ⅔ Grape Soda = Ringo Grape

½ Cola + ½ Orange Soda = Spezi

½ Fruit Punch + ½ Sprite = Sparkle Punch

Get your mouth ready for a burst of sweet, fizzy flavor, but watch out, once you start blending sodas together, you may never want to drink them individually again! Make sure you grab a clean glass each time you blend, and only add ice after you've eyed up the correct measurements! Lastly, some of these sodas contain caffeine, so make sure it's OK with a grown-up before you fill 'er up!

⅔ Fruit Punch   +   ⅓ Lemonade   =   Bug Juice

⅓ Dr. Pepper   +   ⅔ Cola   =   Dr. Cool

½ Orange Soda   +   ½ Cream Soda   =   Orange Dream

½ Fruit Punch   +   ½ Mountain Dew   =   Monster Mash

Pineapple Soda   +   ⅔ Strawberry Soda   =   Snowcone

½ Grape Soda   +   ½ Orange Soda   =   Swamp Water

Gross Out!

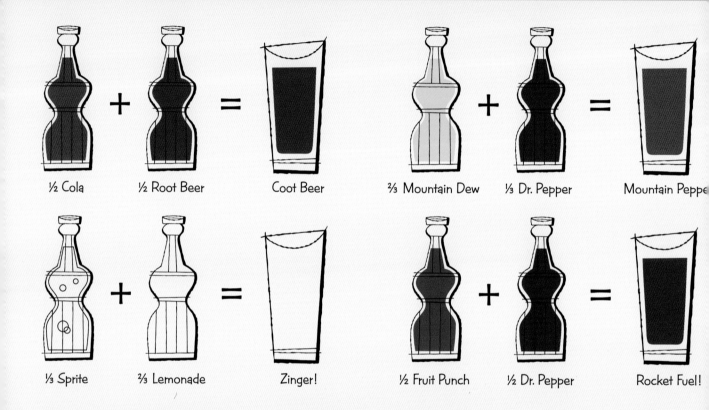

½ Cola + ½ Root Beer = Coot Beer

⅔ Mountain Dew + ⅓ Dr. Pepper = Mountain Peppe

⅓ Sprite + ⅔ Lemonade = Zinger!

½ Fruit Punch + ½ Dr. Pepper = Rocket Fuel!

Prepare yourself for the grossest, gnarliest, most disgusting soda blends in the world! The recipes for these horrible concoctions have been kept locked up for centuries in a secret underground vault, to make sure nobody ever attempts to make them! Only a few adventurous daredevils have every attempted to drink all five of these terrible treats! Consider yourself warned!

THE GRAVEYARD!

There is a legend from long ago about a boy named Fred and his sister Wendy who had a wonderfully awful idea one day while standing at a soda fountain.

They wondered what would happen if you filled a single cup with a splash of every flavor from the fountain. The man behind the counter warned them against it, but they didn't listen. They filled their cups from each fountain, one by one, and once their cups were full they each put their nickel on the counter and left the store. Neither was heard from ever again, and to this day, that blend is known only as...

The Graveyard!

Beware!

Drinks by Name

Metric Conversion Chart

The recipes in this book use US fl oz; this chart converts fl oz to other US measures, and metric milliliters.

cup	oz	tbsp	tsp	ml
1	8	16	48	240
3/4	6	12	36	180
2/3	5	11	32	160
1/2	4	8	24	120
1/3	3	5	16	80
1/4	2	4	12	60
1/8	1	2	6	30
1/16	1/2	1	3	15

Epilogue

We're delighted to have shared our favorite kiddie cocktail recipes with you, and we hope you'll enjoy trying them as much as we enjoyed tasting them with our test kitchen helpers! Each recipe is fun to make, and like anything sweet and delicious, kiddie cocktails are meant to be shared in the company of good friends and family. So invite the gang to join you each time you make a new drink from this book!

We hope that once you've mastered each drink recipe, you'll adjust the ingredients to understand how each of them affects the taste of your drink. We also hope that you'll continue to experiment, and create your very own unique recipes!

Kiddie cocktails are very special, so they should only be enjoyed as an occasional extra treat — perhaps once a week — and only one glass at a time. This way, while you're sipping away, you'll savor every drop and look forward to your next kiddie cocktail!

Always remember, too much of a good thing is never good for you...

Stuart Sandler

Stuart Sandler launched the Font Diner (www.fontdiner.com) font foundry in 1996, inspired by American popular culture of the 1930s–1960s. He has created more than 1,200 original typefaces for the graphic design industry, and solidly established a reputation as the premier retro display typeface designer. In addition to creating new, historical inspired typefaces, Sandler is also focused on the preservation and revival of photolettered cold type with his acquisition of the Filmotype and Lettering, Inc. typeface libraries.

In 2004, Sandler launched Mister Retro (www.misterretro.com), offering retro graphic design software products to complement his original typefaces. Mister Retro features a wildly popular suite of Photoshop plug-ins, Snappy Hour vector artwork, and original serigraphs from the world-renowned lowbrow artist Derek Yaniger. When he's not in his studio, Sandler enjoys life in Eau Claire, Wisconsin, with his family, and indulging in world-class supper club dining — hunkered over a fancy pickle, radish, and black olive relish tray and sipping on a Shirley Temple.

Derek Yaniger

What's buzzin' cousin? Lemme clue ya' to what Derek's been up to these most recent dims n'brights. He's makin' art like... no-tomorrow-style. This cat's got a way long history of scratchin' out art for lots of king-sized bigwigs, like Marvel Comics and Cartoon Network. But nowadays he strictly digs the gigs that let him beat his own bongos.

He gets a large charge creatin' art for a whole heap of way-out events, such as the Tiki Oasis, Las Vegas Rockabilly Weekend, Tales of the Cocktail, and even Spain's Wild Weekend! But what really flips his switches, like... too much, is makin' with the Van Gogh routine. Derek's had his paint splatters hung in galleries all over the world: MondoPop in Italy, Outré in Australia, Vertigo in Mexico, and Castor + Pollux in the UK, to namedrop just a fewsville.

Korero Books released a collection of Derek's retro art entitled Wildsville, The Art of Derek Yaniger, and shortly after, Tiki Mugs, which features a heapin' helpin' of Derek's mid-century tiki art, as well as several tiki mugs he's designed for Tiki Farm and Munktiki.

Check out more of Derek's art online at www.DerekArt.com and get your own at www.misterretro.com!